JI

I'm Going To **READ!**™

These levels are meant only as guides;
you and your child can best choose a book that's right.

Level 1: Kindergarten–Grade 1 . . . Ages 4–6
- word bank to highlight new words
- consistent placement of text to promote readability
- easy words and phrases
- simple sentences build to make simple stories
- art and design help new readers decode text

Level 2: Grade 1 . . . Ages 6–7
- word bank to highlight new words
- rhyming texts introduced
- more difficult words, but vocabulary is still limited
- longer sentences and longer stories
- designed for easy readability

Level 3: Grade 2 . . . Ages 7–8
- richer vocabulary of up to 200 different words
- varied sentence structure
- high-interest stories with longer plots
- designed to promote independent reading

Level 4: Grades 3 and up . . . Ages 8 and up
- richer vocabulary of more than 300 different words
- short chapters, multiple stories, or poems
- more complex plots for the newly independent reader
- emphasis on reading for meaning

LEVEL 2

Library of Congress Cataloging-in-Publication Data Available

2 4 6 8 10 9 7 5 3 1

Published by Sterling Publishing Co., Inc.
387 Park Avenue South, New York, NY 10016
Text copyright © 2005 by Harriet Ziefert Inc.
Illustrations copyright © 2005 by Laura Rader
Distributed in Canada by Sterling Publishing
c/o Canadian Manda Group, 165 Dufferin Street
Toronto, Ontario, Canada M6K 3H6
Distributed in Great Britain and Europe by Chris Lloyd at Orca Book
Services, Stanley House, Fleets Lane, Poole BH15 3AJ, England
Distributed in Australia by Capricorn Link (Australia) Pty. Ltd.
P.O. Box 704, Windsor, NSW 2756, Australia

I'm Going To Read is a trademark of Sterling Publishing Co., Inc.

Printed in China

Sterling ISBN 1-4027-2074-2

Silly Pig

Pictures by Laura Rader

Sterling Publishing Co., Inc.
New York

"Where are you going,
you silly pig?"

"I'm leaving home,"
said silly pig.
"I'm leaving home.
I've grown so big."

"What?
Leaving home,
you silly pig!
You're not so big."

can't

"Where are you going,
you silly pig?"

"I'm going to dig,"
said silly pig.

"What?
Going to dig?
You're not so big.
You can't dig!"

"I can," said silly pig.
"I can dig!"

"Where are you going,
you silly pig?"

"I'm going to drive . . .
to drive a rig.
I'm so big," said silly pig.

"What?
Going to drive?
You can't drive a rig!"

"I can!" said silly pig.
"I can drive a rig!"

store   the

"Where are you going,
you silly pig?"

"I'm going to the store.
I'm going to the store
to buy a wig."

"What?
Going to the store
to buy a wig?
Silly pig!
You don't need a wig."

don't

"Where are you going,
you silly pig?"

"I'm going to a ball
to dance a jig.
I'm going to dance
and wear a wig."

"I'll show you!"
said silly pig.

And he danced . . .

and he danced . . .

and he danced . . .

and he danced . . .
until he fell!

Poor pig!
Poor wig!

"I'm going home,"
said tired pig.
"I don't want to jig!
I don't want a wig!"

"Welcome home,
you tired pig!"

THE END